The Esoteric Structure Of The Alphabet And It's Hidden Mystical Language

Alvin Boyd Kuhn

Kessinger Publishing's Rare Reprints

Thousands of Scarce and Hard-to-Find Books on These and other Subjects!

- Americana
- Ancient Mysteries
- Animals
- Anthropology
- Architecture
- Arts
- Astrology
- Bibliographies
- Biographies & Memoirs
- Body, Mind & Spirit
- Business & Investing
- Children & Young Adult
- Collectibles
- Comparative Religions
- Crafts & Hobbies
- Earth Sciences
- Education
- Ephemera
- Fiction
- Folklore
- Geography
- Health & Diet
- History
- Hobbies & Leisure
- Humor
- Illustrated Books
- Language & Culture
- Law
- Life Sciences
- Literature
- Medicine & Pharmacy
- Metaphysical
- Music
- Mystery & Crime
- Mythology
- Natural History
- Outdoor & Nature
- Philosophy
- Poetry
- Political Science
- Science
- Psychiatry & Psychology
- Reference
- Religion & Spiritualism
- Rhetoric
- Sacred Books
- Science Fiction
- Science & Technology
- Self-Help
- Social Sciences
- Symbolism
- Theatre & Drama
- Theology
- Travel & Explorations
- War & Military
- Women
- Yoga
- *Plus Much More!*

**We kindly invite you to view our catalog list at:
http://www.kessinger.net**

ESOTERIC STRUCTURE OF THE ALPHABET

The modern world is awakening slowly to the fact that in the day we call ancient, though it was but a few thousand years ago in the run of millions, advanced men fully worthy of the name of sages were deeply versed in the profundities of recondite philosophy and possessed knowledge of things both human and divine, and well comprehended the great sciences of both cosmology and anthropology. Evident it is that men of this caliber indited the great Scriptures of ancient religions, which have won and held the reverence of mankind so generally that they have been made the unique objects of religious veneration and the canons of spiritual authority for most of the world over long ages. Indeed the homage paid them has been of the character of worship offered to something regarded as divine. The tradition has prevailed that the Bible authors were in truth men of a divine or semi-divine order, or at least men inspired by a divine afflatus to transmit to mankind the heavenly dictation of sacred truth.

A study of ancient literature, growing more enlightened as it is pursued, is revealing the presence of a definitely formulated and highly organic truth-structure, constituted of the essential elements of a great logical systematization of fundamental *archai*, as the Greek word has it, or principles of a cosmic order of being, expressed in many varied forms of representation everywhere over the field of ancient culture. Primarily, of course, the great wisdom was embodied in tomes of a vast body of literature, a literature so cryptically recondite that its esoteric purport has almost completely eluded the most erudite lucubrations of world scholarship from the ancient day to the present. Indeed it has been the perversions and misinterpretations of that ancient corpus of wisdom that have afflicted the religious consciousness of the world, particularly in the West, with an intellectual befuddlement that approaches the status of a universal dementia for some two millennia.

Not only in the scripts of religion, however, but also in a wide variety of other modes of expression was the wisdom tradition embodied and transmitted. It is found, but always in subtle forms of crypticism, —a feature that has bewildered and befogged all later conclusions of investigators—in ancient art, in architecture, in myth-making, secret society ritual, dramatic scenario, music, mathematics, anthropological science, logic, rhetoric, philosophy, astronomy, astrology, semantics, psychology, festival ordinances, social ceremonies and throughout the warp and woof of life generally. Now, perhaps strangest of all the channels through which it was given expression, comes the momentous revelation that the sagacious genius of antiquity had even insinuated a form of its basic outline into the very structure of that ground-base of all literature, —the *alphabet*. The announcement and elucidation of its presence in this, the fundamental semantic code for the transmission of human thought, should rank as an epochal event in the history of world culture.

Ancient sagacity viewed high spiritual culture in a different light from that in which it is envisaged today. While modern intelligence aims to disseminate its blessings over the widest popular area, hoping that it may edify the mass body of people generally, the sages of old acted upon a different estimate of the possibilities in the case. They appraised the cultural potential of the "vulgar masses" as practically nil, and therefore deemed it a sacrilege to cast the precious jewels of esoteric truth and knowledge to the "swine" that would trample them in the mire of unconscionable crudity of misunderstanding. It may be said that the history of religious cultism over many centuries has demonstrated the practical wisdom of this conservatism. The perversion, corruption, materialization and literalization of the lofty mystical sense of ancient cryptic literature, our power to rightly interpret which is only now being regained, has caused perhaps the most colossal debacle in the culture of spiritual values in the course of known history. Its easily discernible evil fruitage has been the positive derationalization of the Occidental mind as regards all things religious, theological and Scriptural. It has deprived that mind of the cardinal advantage of knowing the sublime meaning of the splendid Jewish-Christian Scriptures, which are a collection of ancient mythographic portrayals of spiritual truth, sadly and calamitously mistaken for history.

Not only were the Sages constrained to adopt methods of crypticism of varied forms to safeguard precious cosmic and anthro-

4

pogenic truth from desecration by the "rabble," but they employed a technique which found its basic authentication in nature itself. As the world below is a mundane reflection and copy of an over-shadowing world of spiritual truth, they strove to portray the structural forms of that higher truth by representing it under the forms of its counterparts everywhere existent in the natural world. Even supposed history was oriented into the form of archetypal ideologies. But everywhere, in drama, ritual, choral dance, festival institution and in language the astute formulators aimed to incorporate their figures of fundamental *archai*. A great structure compounded of the elements of the cosmic logic of creation was inwrought into the pattern of all these modes of human cultural expression. Finally, if not perhaps initially, its structural design was woven into the formation of the alphabet.

If this cryptic organic form was the structural principle determining the arrangement of the alphabet, it must be seen to have made its significance definitely basic in all literature. For thus the words themselves, carrying the elements of the original letter components would constantly represent the forms of the archaic thought which as symbols they portrayed. So that in reconstructing the hidden outlines of meaning form in the alphabet, we are piercing to the heart's core of the most recondite connotations of all literature.

It is a commonplace of present educational theory to say that letters of the alphabet are symbolic representations of the sounds universally possible to the human vocal organs. It is hardly as generally known that in shape they are more than mere algebraic x's or sheer onomatapoetic imitations. They are in fact evident forms shaped to picture basic ideas. They are true ideograms. The capital letter A, for instance, is obviously the cardinal letter I, the symbol of primordial unity (since it is also the number 1), split apart from the top into the creative duality of spirit and matter, the cross-bar indicating the interrelation which dynamically subsists between them. The U (V) symbolizes, exactly as it is drawn, the descent of spirit into matter and its return above. The W pluralizes it, and we find, not strangely, the W to be the letter that pluralizes words in the Egyptian hieroglyphics. The O readily symbolizes the endlessness of matter and of eternity. So that the Gnostics, when they named the unit of deity in the cosmos the IAO, had condensed in the triadic name a sermonette in full, signifying the initial bifurcation of the first unit divine consciousness, the I, apart into the duality, A, and running the round of an eternal cycle, O. And so even *Revelation* has it: "I (am the) A (and the) O, the beginning and the end, the first and the last,"— IAO. (The almost breath-taking significance of the M, when the spirit says "I AM," will be introduced later.)

It is possibly true that literation started with the utilization of the two simplest elements of written symbolism, the vertical line I and the circle O. At any rate it is to be shown here that nearly all divine names in antiquity were built up from and upon these two. For the Egyptians of remote past time had combined the two in the form of what is almost certainly the most ancient of cross symbols, the *crux ansata*, ansated cross, called by them the A N K H (more recently spelled E N K H), an O topping an I with a horizontal line at the point of contact. It represents by the O above, the *endless* existence of that which is the indestructible primordial matter, the eternal Mother of all things; and by the I below, it indicates the emanation of creative mind, or spirit power, from the heart of the great sea of first matter plunging downward. The horizontal bar shows both their conjunction and their separation, as does any boundary line between two areas. But the median line is important also because it marks the meeting point between the two poles of spirit and matter, since it is at this point that all reality is brought out to manifestation through the union of the two. The ANKH is the astrological symbol— ♀.

The two symbols with which literate symbolism begins are thus the I and the O. The item of their gender comes first to notice. The I is masculine, as standing for the Father's power of generation, which is spirit; the O is the eternal feminine, matter, the universal Mother, personalized in ancient religions by such goddesses as Isis, Cybele, Mylitta, Aditi, Venus, Juno and others. The appropriateness of this symbolism from the subsidiary phallic side needs no accentuation, nevertheless is very important and indeed very wonderful. (The author has fully dealt with it in his larger work, SEX AS SYMBOL.) As all progenation of life can come only through the union of male and female elements of the cosmic duality, a symbol that would dramatize *life* would have to combine both the I and the O. This the Egyptians did in their great A N K H symbol, which thus is their written word for *life*, and carries also the connotation of two other elements entering into life, or

6

necessary for life, namely *love* and *tie*. Even more than the IAU it condenses in its three renderings the gist of a mighty sermon, and becomes the hieroglyph of both the structure and the meaning of life. Rendered in one sentence the symbol means *life* because life can exist only where two things, spirit (I), and matter (O), are *tied* together by a sufficiently cohesive power, *love*. Love ties the two together to procreate life. The A N K H is therefore the first and greatest symbol in the world, which should make us aware that the cross is the first and greatest symbol because it is the symbol of *life* and *not* of death. (The ancients said, however, that the soul, when incarnated in the body on earth, was in its spiritual "death," and therefore the cross became the emblem of death— but soul-death, not body-death—a death viewed wrongly by all theology since the days of ancient mystery teaching, since the reference is to the "dead" condition of the *soul* when immersed in body, and not to the demise of the physical body. Even in this view it equally connoted *life*, for it was the soul's relative "death" that gave life to the creature, whose bodily demise in turn liberated it for its freer life above.)

Detaching the two emblems from each other as they are united in the A N K H symbol, and combining them in lateral juxtaposition, we have the first divine word and name in all literature, IO. That it figures with equally fundamental significance in ancient typological numerology is evident from the fact that the two, now converted into numbers, constitute the cardinal base of all mathematics, the number 10. Modern study seems not to have recognized the close connection, amounting almost to identity, between the letters of the alphabet as originally devised, and numbers. Numbers were indicated by letters. Each letter carried a number value. Hence words were composed of those alphabetical units that would together express an idea, a mental value, but as well a numerical value. As far as the Scriptures are concerned, even whole sentences were constructed to total a number quantity. As Pythagoras had said, God geometrized in creating the world; he built the universe on number. Such esoteric works as *The Zohar*, of ancient Jewish Kabalistic literature, reveal clearly also that the deity formed the creation by means of the letters of the alphabet. This can have sense only on the predication that as (according to the Scriptures) he spake and the worlds formed themselves in order under the vibratory impact of the letter tones

7

of his voice, every letter sound of the creative reverberation became a constituent element in the cosmic framework. Every letter expressed or in fact constituted a principle or fundamental part of the universal structure. Perhaps this is one of the great lost keys to our recovery of the cryptic purport of ancient writing.

The archaic IO (10) then would be charged with the potency of the first projection of the creative thought-force, but only in its first partition into duality, not in its later and further subdivision. In its expression as the prime triplicity it was the IAO (which became IAH and JAH), and its still further differentiation toward endless multiplicity at the quaternary stage brought it to the form of the great Tetragrammaton, the Kabalistic J H V H. In its full seven-letter expression it became, on the side of matter alone, the seven-vowelled name, composed of the seven primary vowel sounds made by the human voice. The Greek alphabet still retains seven vowels, a, short e, long e, i, short o, long o and u. This was to express the fact that every cycle of creation runs through seven sub-cycles, each of which sounds out the reverberation of one of the seven successive component form-tones.

The potent symbol, typifying primogenital creative energy of mind and matter combined in the relation of polarity, being the power that dominated all things as it was their creator, became the figure of all combined mental and material ruling power everywhere, as all lesser ruling units were themselves but projected partial rays of the power itself. It was therefore the first *king* in the cosmic realm, as every divided segment of it was king in the tinier realm over which it exercised sovereignty. How notable this will appear when we shall see in a moment that the very word, *King*, derives from the A N K H name!

Nothing has been more revealing than the list of words, in English, Greek, German, Hebrew, which can be traced to the old Egyptian name of this mighty symbol. Its central idea, it was noted, is the production of life through the tieing or *union* of spirit and matter. The central clue to the meaning of all these derivatives is the idea of *tieing* two things together. It must be elucidated that in building words upon the A N K H stem, the H may be virtually dropped out of consideration, as K H is equally well expressed by K alone. But K H is also equivalent to C H, which often replaces it. The vowel A is of inconsequential value and can also be dropped. So there is the bare N K left as the hard root.

The next matter to be noted is that in later philological usage it was immaterial whether it was written N K or K N. And in Greek the N K (K N) became N G (G N),—a significant item. With these specifications it is possible now to discern a whole new world of meaning in many common words never deemed to have come down from so divine a lineage.

It is seen first in such words as *anchor*, that which *ties* a boat to a fixed place; *knit, knot, link, gnarled, gnaw, gnash* (accounting for the odd spelling); *ankelosis*, a growing together of two bones; *anger, anguish, anxiety*, a tightening up of feelings. But most interestingly it seems to have given name to at least four joints or hinge-points (*hinge* itself seems to be another) in the human body: *ankle, knee, neck* and *knuckles*. *Lung*, as being the place where outside air unites with the inner blood, could perhaps be added. Far away as our English *join* appears to be from a source in A N K H, (N being the only letter common to both), it is certainly directly from it after all. For A N K H was the root of the Latin *jungo*, to *join*, N K becoming N G through the Greek. From this we get *junction, adjunct, juncture, conjunction*, from the Latin past participle form of *jungo*, —*junctus*. But in coming into English through the French, all these words were smoothed down to *join, joint*, and this carried so far into English as to give us finally *union*, which is really *junction* in its primal form. With even the N dropping out we have *yoke*, that which *ties* two oxen together. And in Sanskrit it comes out as *yoga*, which in reality stands for *yonga*, meaning *union*.

The English present participle ending -*ing*, as well as the prefix *con-*, meaning *with* or *together*, likely comes from the A N K H. For the —*ing* connotes a continuing of things moving on together. Therefore all three parts of the word *con-nect-ing* would be from the ancient word.

Our most common word, *thing*, likewise comes from A N K H, as a thing is that which is created by the union of spirit and matter, a divine conception and atomic substance.

Next comes one that carries an impressive significance in the study, the common verb to *know*, in Greek *gnosco*, German *kennen*, English *ken*. What constitutes the knowing act? The *joining* together of two *things*, consciousness and an object of consciousness, for there must be something apart from consciousness to be known. So Greek called *knowledge* the *Gnosis*. The Greek verb meaning

9

to be, *gignomai*, also has the G N, as token that existence is the result of the "*ankhing*" together of spirit and matter.

But a most surprising Hebrew derivation from A N K H is the first-personal pronoun, I. It is in fact the A N K H itself unchanged except for the inconsequential insertion of two minor vowels o and i, making it ANOKHI. This is amazingly significant, since it reveals the identity of the innermost soul-being of man, the I ego, with the primal cosmic mind. That consciousness in man which enables him to think and say "I" is indeed a unit element of that same cosmic mind. In the I-consciousness of a creature the central creative mind energy of the universe is nucleated in unity. And as the ruler of all life in every domain, it is in that function and capacity the *king* of life! That power which *knows things* is verily creation's *king*. And also then it must be the power that *thinks*. Gerald Massey, great scholar of ancient occult knowledge, connects in kindred significance *think* and *thing*, a thing being that which has been thought by some mind. The I, as the *king* of consciousness, both *thinks* and *knows*. The German has for king *Koenig*, the one who *can*, (which in German is *koennen*) and the one who *knows* what is best. And what has the Greek for *king*? Astonishingly *anax*, which is equivalent to the spelling *anaks*.

The Greek for *messenger*, one who *ties* the sender with the recipient of a message, is *angelos*, from which is our *angel*. And *messenger* itself has the *ng* in it. Where two lines meet we have an *angle*. A *nook* suggests something in the A N K H meaning. Perhaps hundreds more words might be traced from this venerable but most significant origin in the A N K H. And the words themselves help us reestablish the fundamental elements in the composition and structure of the great ancient knowledge so well called the *Gnosis*.

The letter I, as the spiritual-masculine first half of the great IO symbol, must be examined more closely. It is in the alphabet and in language the symbol of the divine mind principle. It is the *king* of all being, knowing, determining, ordering, acting. And so it has been made the *10th* (tenth) letter of the Hebrew alphabet, the king number both 1 and 10 or any multiple thereof, and therefore has for its meaning the word *God* itself. Its Hebrew name is YOD (YODH) and means the "hand of God." Its hieroglyphic representation is that of a tongue of candle flame, bent as it would be momentarily if blown upon by a gentle puff of the breath. This is to indicate the breathing of God upon the latent creative fires of atomic energy to blow them up to creative heat. It is suggested in *Genesis* when it is said that God brooded over the great deep. Water is the symbol of matter, as matter in the cosmos and water on the earth are the common universal mothers of life. And matter contains the latent atomic fire which creates all. God blows upon this latent fire to enflame it for creative work. This is indicated in the bent candle flame of the YOD, —᾽.

Ten is esoterically called the "perfect number." In the highest possible sense it is the number that rounds out or perfects a cycle of creation, and it does this through the interrelation of the eternal upper triad of noumenal creative forces, cosmic spirit-soul-mind, with the septenate of lower physical energies, as anciently represented in the great system of Egyptian Gnosis, and faithfully reproduced in the Ten Holy Sephiroth of the early Jewish Kabalah. The YOD then stands for that divine creative fire that in its deployment as a decanate of powers, forges the worlds into the shape prefigured in the divine mind. The triple-aspected cosmic Noumenon designs the blueprint of the creation-to-be, and the seven hierarchical energies carry them out in the world of concreteness. If one reflects on the remarkable physical phenomenon of a ray of white light passing through a triadic glass prism and casting the refracted rays upon a screen in the seven colors of the spectrum, one will have an instructive analogue of the number basis of the creation. *Revelation* symbolism evidently represents it as the Beast with seven heads and ten horns, the three horns in excess of the number of heads being presumably in the invisible noumenal worlds, the heavens of pure thought.

Concomitant with the IO primacy in symbolism runs a variant representation which depicts successive stages in the creative process. It begins with the symbol of inchoate matter, the O as representing primordial inorganic homogeneity or the unity and eternity of life in its unmanifest state. It in fact typifies what to us stands as empty space. It is empty (to us) as exhibiting absolutely nothing in visible palpable form. "The world was without form and void." But to the cosmic consciousness it is doubtless not empty, since it is filled with substance apperceptible to that consciousness. What it seems to us is best depicted by the empty circle, —O.

The next stage shows the circle with the visible point in the center. This design indicates the emergence of the first organic ntification out of unmanifest being, —⊙.

The third depiction shows the circle cut horizontally into two halves, upper and lower, by the median diameter line, —⊖. This diagram shows the bifurcation of the original unity into the creative duality and the polarization of its two self-contained opposite natures, a prerequisite for any creation of visible organic worlds.

The fourth stage indicates the opposition or crossing of the forces of the two ends of the polarity of spirit and matter, or the cross within the circle, the vertical line standing for the spirit force and the horizontal for the physical. Lifting the cross out of the circle, we have it in its simplest form, and since life can *add* increase unto itself only by this crossing of spirit and matter, the cross becomes the sign of *addition*, the plus sign, —⊕.

The fifth stage has the same configuration, but as it were, turned one-eighth on its axis, giving the X within the circle. This is to show that motion has been introduced, that creation has begun, —⊗. This, similarly to the bent candle flame of the YOD, indicates that God's impulse has begun to move. Then, as the initial motion imparted to the creation not only *adds* to its working potential, but vastly *multiplies* it, the X becomes the sign of multiplication. In this final form the design eventuates in giving us the great symbol of the number 10, —X. And then if we take the X out of its eternal encirclement in the absolute existence— and by the beginning of the movement this emergence is indicated, —and place the two great symbols side by side, we have astonishingly that mystic word and symbol that enters so mysteriously into Scriptural allegory, —the word OX. (The elucidation of the esoteric intimation of this word is reserved for the finale.)

The extensive list of divine names derived from the IO base may now be scanned. Io is itself the name of one of the goddesses with whom Zeus, king of the gods in the Greek pantheon, entered into an escapade that exoterically sounds less honorable than would be expected of divine royalty. But as paramour of the supreme God she would stand in the role of the great Mother of life, like Cybele, Isis and the rest. An Io character occurs in other mythologies.

As, however, the I functions as the male-spiritual symbol and is not to be taken as the vowel force alone, but rather as the consonantal force, it was paired with each of the vowels in turn to represent the conjoined duality. And so we find IA, IE and IU standing as the base of a number of early deific names. The IA came to serve as the final syllable of all names of countries, as Germania, Britannia, Australia, Russia, Austria, Scandanavia, Asia, India, Arabia and many more. The IE begins the original Greek name Iesous (Jesus). Preceded by the H, denoting again the first motion of the breath of God, it began some Greek words for divinity, principally *hieros*, *sacred*, *holy* and a *priest*, from which comes *hierophant*, *hierarchy* and the old Greek name for Jerusalem, *Hierosolyma*.

But as IU it stands as one of the most basic of all divine name-forms. IU was in fact the shortest and commonest of Egyptian verbs, and meant *to come*. Because the divine nature was considered an element of consciousness that was in course of its evolutionary coming to deify mankind, the Messiah doctrine connoted the idea of the slow, gradual and continuous *coming* of the deific mind in the world. In fact a common name in Egypt for the Messianic character was "the Comer." "Iu is he who comes regularly and continually," periodically. Hence IU is the primal Egyptian name of deity. As such it formed the first element of the great compound Egyptian name of the Christ-Messiah, *Iu-em-hetep*, which was shortened by the Greeks into *Imhotep*. In full translation this would read: *Iu* (he who comes) *-em* (with) *-hetep* (peace, also seven); "he who comes with peace as number seven." This name comprehends in itself another great sermon like the A N K —symbol, referring to the occult fact that in any cycle of creation the principle of divine consciousness that will unfold to bring *peace* to the chaotic subconscious elements (the so-called six elementary powers, the potencies in the atom) *comes* to full outward expression in the *seventh* and last round of the cycle. Christhood is always a seventh unfoldment. Our own word *seven* comes from *hetep*, as this shortened to *hept*, and directly became the Latin *sept-em*, by the interchange of h with s, as occurs in very many instances, as in *Asura* becoming *Ahura*. H and s are also closely related through the Hebrew letter *shin*, which is either S or sh in sound. S is really only a sharper h.

The next step in the development is quite notable. The I being male-spiritual, a consonant (masculine gender) rather than a vowel, and representing the projected ray of divine mind that

13

beamed forth out of primordial being, ran the course of its projection into the deepest bosom of matter, planted its germinal seed in matter's womb, then *turned to return*, the configuration of the I was changed or enlarged to include in its shape the suggestion of the turning upward for the return. It might most significantly then be said that it was *turned* into the letter J. With more definiteness the J-form could bespeak the masculine-divine than the vowel-feminine or the androgynous aspect. Also in this form it could be more fitly prefixed to the other vowels, as JA, JE, JO and JU. With this important change the number of divine names begins to multiply exceedingly.

It is impossible to pass by this item of the turning of the I into the J (the two are essentially the same letter still in Latin) without calling attention to the astonishing significance of the fact in relation to one of the key words in the Biblical allegory of the soul's descent *and return*. In the Hebrew-Mosaic allegory in the Old Testament the place where God descended in a cloud to meet and commune with his children (Israel) was Mount Sinai. This name then must mean the lowest point to which the spirit-soul descends to meet matter, the pivot point round which it swings to begin its return to the heavens. This is diagramed by the lower turn of the J. What must be our astonishment, then, to discover that this key name Sinai derives from the Egyptian word *seni* (*senai*), meaning *"point of turning to return!"* And where, in concrete reality, is that point located? Nowhere else than in the physical body of man! The physical body of man is the Mount Sinai of the Bible. And where else could God and man meet than in the body of his human child? An obscure point in scholarship has at last come forth to enlighten us on one of the most important features of our sacred Scriptures.

Greek mythology gives us Jason, a divine figure. In the Old Testament we have Jacob, Jabez, Jared, Jakin and perhaps others; James in the New; Jacques, Jack, a folk-lore character of the deity in man; Janus, definitely a Christ-figure in Roman mythology. The JE-form gives Jesus, Jesse, Jeshua, Jeshu, Jezebel, Jeremiah, Jerusalem, Jehu, Jethro, Jehosophat, Jehovah, Jephthah, and others. In passing it seems quite worth while to analyze the true context of the name Jesus. It is the JE combined with the Egyptian SU, meaning *son, heir, prince*, successor to the king; and the final masculine terminal letter, which was F in Egyptian, but became S (US) in Latin: JE-SU-S. It would then mean the coming masculine-divine son (of God the Father) as "prince of peace." The masculine terminal F of Egypt was kept in the variant form JO-SE-F, JO-SE-PH, as in the Russian Yussuf at the present. This is the most prominent in the JO group, which includes Joram, Josiah, Joash, Jonah (Jonas), Job, Joses, Joachim, Joel, Joshua and (in the Norse) Jotun. These have never been recognized for the divine names they are, because of the inveterate mistaking of Old Testament allegorism for assumed factual history. But, being in the allegory of man's divinity immersed in the flesh, they are incontestably the names of the divine or Christly principle personalized in the many myth-forms. Horus, the Christ of Egypt, had for one of his designations "the Jocund."

The JU-form yields Judah, Judas, Judea, Jubilee, Judith, Julia, along with significant common noun derivatives such as *judge, jury, justice*. But Latin mythic usage exalted the JU to the very highest pinnacle of divine dignity in naming its supreme deity after the Egyptian JU, adding the word for *father, pater (piter)*, to it to form the great name of the king of the gods, JU-PITER. Even the god's wife and sister partook of the glorious title— JUNO. The great Caesar boasted of his fabled derivation from deity in his cognomen Julius. The Juniper tree carries this connection with divine source. Latin *juventus*, our "youth," conveys the idea that the gods are ever *young*. (The I, the J and Y are all forms of the same letter-sound.) From this we have our *junior*, the German has *jung*, meaning and pronounced as our *young*. The *ju*—that begins the Latin *jungo (iungo)*, to *join*, indicates that spirit and matter are joined together anew to generate fresh life. This IU (JU) stem is much more significant than has ever been seen before. In the form of YU—it enters into the great word signifying the birth of deity—*Yule*.

Every letter, of course, expresses some aspect or segment of creative purpose. Alphabetical schematism has been presented in several different formulations. In the Hebrew alphabet there were said to be three "mother letters," *aleph* (A), *mem* (M) and *shin* (SH). These ostensibly represent respectively the pre-creation stage (A), the middle stage of spirit's involvement in matter (M), and its final stage of glorious deification (SH), —the symbol of *fire*. M is the symbol of *water*. Life emanates out of potential *fire*, is "baptized" for evolutionary purposes in water, the symbol of matter, and returns to source with fiery potentialities actualized by having "overcome" the powers in the water-matter. The Hebrew word for *fire* is *esh*, and spirit evolves its divine fire in man, *ish*. The divine fire in man made him the *ish*-man, and the divine man in the tribal life of some nations was called the *shaman*.

How the other letters were grouped in relation to the three mother-letters is matter of uncertainty. Several schematic designs have been suggested by students of Kabalism. But two consonants, beside J, were made the central frame of another extensive run of divine names. These are R and L. The names derived from or based on them must be listed.

It is evident that, as their usage worked out, R and L may be regarded as essentially the same letter. The Chinese confusion of the two is well known. But their identification became almost a necessity in the ancient Hebrew-Egyptian exchange of words, ideas and symbols, inasmuch as the Egyptian alphabet had no L and was forced to substitute R in all words where the Hebrew could use either L or R. It is therefore extremely likely that the great basic words, as seen so well in Latin *rex*, *king*, and *lex*, *law*, are of practically identical significance. The heavenly king is the Lord, and the old Saxon derivation of Lord from *law-ward*, as Ruskin points out, is more than coincidental. The king's will was the law in all archaic life, and in theology it is still true that the will of the Lord is the law of life.

Just why R and L came, with J and SH to emblemize divinity is not too clear. They, along with M and N, are of the class of letters called liquids: they are sounded with a continued *flow* of the voice. They could thus have been chosen as representing the on-flowing course of all life. This idea would not have been inappropriate. It may be the correct one. At any rate R came to its divinest application in being chosen as the name of that greatest of all spiritual deities of antiquity, the Egyptian Sun-god *Ra*, whose symbol is that of the sun, the circle with the dot in the center. A cursory view of names based on R and L yields many interesting items. The R and L can be associated with any of the vowels and can either follow or be preceded by it.

From AL-LA we note *Allah*, *Aladdin*, *Alheim* (Elohim), the frequent *Al*—of Arabic names and a host of others, perhaps our *all*. From EL-LE we have *El*, the Hebrew word for *God*, the plural being *Elohim*. The masculine article, *the*, in the four languages derived from Latin, is, as in the Spanish, *el*, and in the French, *le*. This will not be seen as significant until it is recognized that the definite article is, or was, itself a *cognomen of deity*. Spanish *the* is the Hebrew word for *God*, EL. English *the* is the Greek for *God*, *the-os*. And Greek masculine form of *the* is *ho*, a Chinese word for deity. The ancients habitually prefixed *the* to divine names, as "the Osiris."

From IL comes the Arabic Ilbrahim and the Latin *ille*, meaning *this, that which is*, a succinct definition for deity. The Latin name for the sacred tree was the holm-oak, and its Latin name was *ilex*. OL and UL yield a few words referring to divine things. Hebrew *olam*, the *world, eternity*, the *aeon*, and *olah, up*, to *go up*, and the Mohammedan *Ullah, Abdullah*, may trace origin from these two bases.

AR-RA shows in numerous words, *ar* meaning *river* in Hebrew, and there are several rivers on the world map named the *Ar*, or *Arar*. The stream of divine force emanating from the heart of being to create worlds was called the *river*. Every ancient land had its sacred river. As *Ra* was the great solar deity, the origin of *ray, radiant, radius, radium, radiate* and *array* is evident. As the king was the one radiant with divine glory, the *rex* (*rey, roi, roy*), such words as *regal, royal, real* (as in Mont-real), *regulate* (along with *lex, legal, loyal, leal* and *legislate*), are traceable to this source.

Plato has the famous "myth of Er," a divine character. The Greek has *Er-* with the masculine singular ending *-os*, giving the great God of divine love, *Eros*. *Re* must be the base of the common Latin word for *thing, res*, the stem of which is just *re*. This gives *reality, realize* and *reify*, and the prefix denoting *r*epetition, *re-*, as life is constantly repeating its processes; as in *re-new, re-vive, re-store*, etc.

IR-RI shows scant usage, but in OR-RO and UR-RU we encounter a prolific wealth of derivatives, all pointing to high, if not directly divine reference. It is significant, to begin with, that OR is found to be the base of words in several languages meaning two things, *gold* and *light*. French for gold is *or*, and Latin *aur-um*; our word *ore*; Hebrew for *light* is *Oroh*. Gold, the indestructible, was symbolically related to light, which is also indestructible. The creative energy of God flowed forth as light like a golden river, so that all three, *gold, light* and *river* show the derivation from *ar, aur, or*. *Aurora*, God of Dawn, needs no further explication; *aura* and *aureole* likewise.

(UR reveals a grand list of shining names. It was in itself the greatest and most likely the original word for *fire*. The Egyptians, wishing to name it *the* fire, added the divine article, *the*, which in their language was the hieroglyph for the letter P. This addition made it *p-ur-*, *pur*, the Greek word for fire to this day. From this comes *pure*, *purge*, *purgatory*, as also *pyre*, *pyrotechnic* and *empyrean*, the Greek U changing to Y in English, as in hundreds of words. *Ur* (a variant of *aur*, *or*) was the name of that state of the primordial spiritual "fire" from which the first divine ray, Ab-*ra*-ham, proceeded as first father of spiritual Israel (not the historical Hebrews). In the same category it was the name of the universal Egyptian symbol of creative fire, the *uraeus*, "a serpent of fire," which was sevenfold as typifying the seven archangels that created the universe. It is therefore another representation of the dragon or beast with seven heads. Is it strange that our modern discovery of the creative fire of the universe in the atom has brought into prominence as the most fiery of the elements those two whose names incorporate both the title of the Sun-god and the Uraeus, RAdium and URanium? The German language has some hundreds of words prefixing UR, as *Ursprung*, *Urquelle*, *Ursache*, all meaning original source-spring of being. All life came out of UR, the primordial fount of cosmic fire. A verse in the *Chaldean Oracles* says that "all things are the product of one primordial fire, every way resplendent." How resplendent it is our modern nuclear physics is now revealing! The Hebrew word for *father* being *ab*, *Ab-ra-m* is "Father Ra," as clearly as Hebrew can say it. *Ram* would be this creative fire immersed in water, matter.

The list so far traced becomes more than doubled through the prefixing onto these root-forms the Hebrew article, *the*, which is just the letter H. The addition of the H has the force of divinizing the word, as has been seen. So from HAL there is *hallow*, *hale*, *hallel* (Hebrew *to praise*), *halleluiah*, *hail* and more. From HEL can be traced *heal*, *health*, *heil* (German *hail*), *hell* (German, *bright*, *clear*), and most significantly, the Greek *helios*, the sun! The spiral, or *helix*, was a figure tracing the spiraling course of the sun, or its planets around it. The feminine names *Helen*, *Helena* (with the H intensified into S becoming the name of the moon, *Selene*), are assumed to derive from it also. The Greeks adopted unto themselves the divine name *Hellenes*, signifying "bright and shining ones," dubbing the rest of humanity "barbarians." (They did this in the same fashion and with the same motive as the Jews adopted for themselves the divine name *Israelites*, dubbing the rest of mankind "Gentiles.")

From HIL comes doubtless our word *hill*, "the hill of the Lord," the high locale of divine power. (*Har* in the R-group is the Hebrew word for *hill!*)

From the HOL stem comes of course *holy, whole, holism*. Few of particular divine character or reference derive from HUL.

The H-R group yields many of exalted significance. HAR gives *heart, hearth, Har-Tema,* (a name of Horus, the great Christ of Egypt), Harpocrates, (another Greek-Egyptian Christ-name), perhaps *harvest, harp, harpy* (the harpies of Virgil's *Aeneid*). HER gives a long list: *hero* (title of one grade of deities in Greek mythology), German *Herr* (God), *herald, Hera,* (Juno's Greek name), *Heracles* (*Hercules*), *Hermes* (Mercury), and, reinforcing the e with the i, *hieros,* Greek for *sacred.*

HIR appears perhaps in the German for *shepherd,* and in *Hiram.* HOR gives the base of perhaps the greatest of ancient personalizations of Christhood, the Egyptian god *Horus,* who stands on the *horizon, hour, horology, hormone, horn, horticulture. Horn* was a universal ancient symbol of divine power. HUR shows in *Ben-Hur* and *hurricane,* the natural exemplification of divine fiery power. The *Hurrians* were a people sharing Asia Minor with the Hittites.

As H comes out often in the roughened form of CH (KH), and also exchanges often with S, the H-basis of hundreds of words, all in one way or another intimating deific reference, the derivative field is vastly extended, embracing such words as *chalice, charity, care, cure, cross, cheer, choir, chorus, Christos, charm, cherish, cherubim, Serapis, seraphim, sir, sire, seer, ser* (Egyptian for *chief, elder, sire*), *kherufu* (Egyptian for the two lion-gods on the *horizon*).

These lists are put down almost at random. It is certain that intensive research would immensely increase the total number, and no doubt others of the greatest importance could be revealed.

These formations from the basic IO are of the greatest interest and importance. They do not, however, give any intimation of the organic structure in the alphabet which this work is intended to disclose. But they will appear in clearer light as that hidden structure is outlined.

To enforce the cryptic significance of the disclosure now to be made, it is necessary to present, with the utmost brevity, the fundamental meaning-graph of all ancient religious literature. The Bibles of antiquity have but one theme: *the incarnation*. The vast body of ancient Scripture discoursed on but one subject, —the descent of souls, units of deific Mind, sons of God, into fleshly bodies developed by natural evolution on planets such as ours, therein to undergo an experience by which their continued growth through the ranges and planes of expanding-consciousness might be carried forward to ever higher grades of divine being. These tomes of "Holy Writ" therefore embodied their main message in the imagery of *units of a fiery spiritual nature plunging down into water*, the descending souls being described as sparks of a divine cosmic *fire*, and the bodies they were to ensoul being constituted almost wholly of *water*. (The human body is seven-eighths water!)

It can indeed be said that the one sure and inerrant key to the Bibles is the simple concept of fire plunging into water, the fire being spiritual mind-power and water being the constituent element of physical bodies, —as well as the symbol of matter. Soul (spirit) as fire, plunged down into body, as water, and therein had its *baptism*. Hence soul's incarnation on earth was endlessly depicted and dramatized as its crossing a body of water, a Jordan River, Styx River, Red Sea, Reed Sea. Since the water element of human bodies is the "sea" which the soul of fire has to cross in its successive incarnations, and it is red in color, the "Red Sea" of ancient Scriptures is just the human body blood. When the red fire of spirit-soul was gradually introduced into and permeated the original sea-water which was the bodily essence of earliest living creatures on earth, it changed colorless salt water into its own color, red. The "Red Sea" never could have meant anything other than the human blood. The Scriptures reiterate that "fire descended from heaven and turned the sea into blood." This transformation of course took place in man's body, not in the world oceans. This is a clarification that alone can reillumine all old Scriptures with a flashing new and enlightening orientation of meaning. Egypt said that souls came down to "kindle a fire in the sea," to "create a burning within the sea," verily to set the ocean on fire. This has actually been done, but in man's veins and in his passions, not in the seven seas.

It is now to be announced that the great meaning-structure discovered in the alphabet outlines this descent of soul-fire into water and its return to its native empyrean. If one arranges the letters in a circular arc downward from A to the last letter of the first half of the alphabet, and then begins the upward return with the first letter of the second half and completes the arc to the final letter, describing the *lower* half of a circle, one will have blueprinted the organic structure here revealed. On the thesis just presented, one would challenge the claim of such a structure to demonstrate that the first letter or letters were somehow charactered as *fire*, and the two middle letters at the bottom or turning-point of the semi-circle were charactered as *water*. We are proclaiming that the structure meets that challenge and therefore proves itself as true and correct. The result is that, along with every other symbolic device of ancient meaning-form, even the alphabet embodied the central structure of all ancient literature, —the incarnation, the baptism of fire-soul in and under body-water. If this is to be confirmed, we must find *fire* at the top or beginning of the descending arc, and *water* at the bottom or turning-point. It must now be shown that the conditions our thesis requires to prove itself are precisely met in the alphabet. The discovery was made and certified when it was perceived that *the alphabet did fulfill these precise conditions.* The top or beginning letters are A and B, and should, the A alone or combined with B, represent *fire;* the middle letters coming at the base of the arc are M and N, and, *mirabile dictu,* they represent *water!* From A to M, then, the descending arc traces the downward or involutionary plunge of fire into water, reaching its lowest depth with M; from N back to the final letter, whatever it be in different languages, the upward return arc represents the arising out of water and the return through evolution of the heavenly fire to its true home, completing the cycle.

The fire-character of A and B does not show out in such explicit form as does the water-character of M and N. Nevertheless it is intimated and implicit in various ways. The celestial fire emanated from primal source as one ray, but soon radiated out in triadic division, and finally reached the deepest heart of matter in a sevenfold segmentation. But in its first stage of emanation it was always pictured as triform. The YOD candle-flame being its type-form, the Hebrews constructed their letter which was to represent the fire-principle with three YODS at the top level, with lines extending downward to a base, on which all three met and were conjoined in one essence. This gives us the great fire-letter SH, *shin*, —ש .

But the triform fire symbol was only possible as the result of the one first ray bifurcating into the *two* fires of spirit and matter and uniting to generate their product, which became the third aspect. Therefore if a word was to be constructed to embody the two-flame aspect as preceding the three-flame form, it would have to be of two letters, the first being a letter representing the two-fire stage, and the other the letter *shin*, the three-fire aspect. And what letter is it that depicts the two-flame stage, the first real creative stage? Precisely what the thesis calls for—the first letter *aleph*, composed of *two YODS*, one above, the other below, the central axis, a slightly variant form of our mathematical sign of division, a horizontal line with a dot above and one below it. All life is an interplay between the upper fire of spirit and the lower fires of sense and the flesh, of "pure" fire in air and "impure" fire in water. Even the English A carries the same depiction, as it represents the one vertical line of spirit raying downward, the I, as being split apart into duality, with the two separated lines still connected by the horizontal bar of mutual inter-relation, —א .

The resulting Hebrew word, then, for *fire* is just what the specifications of symbolic representation demand. The word should be composed of symbolic letters carrying the idea of the one-fire, the dual fire and the triple fire signs, and this is precisely what the Hebrew word for *fire* is. It is ESH, really AeSH, composed of *aleph*, subvowelled by e, and *shin*. *Aleph* is the dual letter, *shin* the triple, and the middle bar between the two YODS in the *aleph* is the single-bar *fire*. Then significantly *man*, who embodies this single, double and triple *fire* is ISH!

One would ask at once whether the English word *ash* would carry the same connotations, being the visible end result of fire. It is extremely likely that it does. Not only is it at once evident in its relation to fire as its residue, —ashes, —but the Norse mythology, depicting the radiating streams of the living fire under the imagery of a branching tree, chose the *ash* as the tree-type of the fiery emanation: *Ygdrasil*, the ash-tree of life.

It has already been stated that the patriarchal character designated as Abram personified in the Hebrew formulations the first *father* of spiritual life, emanating out of the primordial essence of fire, UR of the Chasdim. (This latter word signifies not national Chaldeans, as those thus designated were not an ethnic group, but a spiritual caste. The term stands for the first archangels, or creative fires, the seven.) To be the father of spiritual life in an evolutionary cycle, this ray had to be the first aspect of the emanation. Therefore it would be found to be composed of the first two letters of the alphabet. This is precisely what is found in the Hebrew word for *father*: AB. Linking it with the Egyptian RA, the radiant solar deity, we have AB-RA-M, receiving later in its evolution the developed powers of godhood represented by the fifth Hebrew letter, *he*, and so becoming AB-RA-H-AM. And as Abram came out of the primordial empyreal fire, UR, it is hardly coincidental that even UR begins with that letter, U, which (with V) represents the downward line of descent, the turning upward and the return to the heights

The detailed knowledge is not at present available to trace the chain of linked steps in the descent of the divine flame from A down to M. It does not seem apparent that at any rate in extant alphabets there is to be found a sequence of letter significations paralleling and depicting the successive stages of the creative fire's descent into the water, or matter involvement. If such an explicit arrangement was planned for the first alphabets, it seems impossible to trace the stages in orderly succession in present alphabets. But what emerges with astonishing certitude is that the central letters, M and N, carry the significance of what the diagram demands, —*water*. Thus at the point of lowest descent, where our thesis requires water, there indeed we have it.

Every letter of the Hebrew alphabet, beside carrying a number value, also has attached to it a symbolic monograph: B is *beth* and means *house*; G is *gimel* and means *camel*; D is *daleth* and means *door*; H is *he* and means *window*, etc. When we come to M, we find it is named *mem* and means—*water*! N is called *nun* and means that which is the animal life in water, —*fish*! This is in the Hebrew. But amazingly, when we turn to the old Egyptian, we find that N has the name of *nun* likewise, but means and is the hieroglyph of —*water*! Its character letter is simply a short line indented to indicate *seven waves*, as our English script *m* is a succession of three waves. M therefore in the Hebrew, and in English as well, marks the nadir of soul's descent into water, and N, at the same level and therefore also signifying water (or as *fish* the organic life in water), marks the turning-point for return, the Mount Sinai of evolution. Its reference is undoubtedly to this earth, which true symbolic insight discovers is itself—and not any hill on its surface—the "mount" or "hill of the Lord," on which God meets man in a cloud of fire, and on which all sermons are preached by his inner deity to man, and all temptations, crucifixions, spiritual initiations and final transfigurations take place.

From A, the point of emanation of the spiritual fire, the creative stream of living energy, the river of vivification, as the Greeks called it, proceeded and swept downward until at M it had immersed its fiery potencies in the water of the human body, therein to begin to do its evolutionary work of kindling its own bright flame of spiritual consciousness in the red sea of the human blood. And now it is known that this red blood was originally sea water. As fire causes water to evaporate, the ancient allegorism represented the divine fire as drying up the water of the bodily sea, permitting souls to pass over the watery terrain dryshod. Variant symbolism had the Christ nature walking on the water without sinking into its depths. Egyptian figurism had the fire causing the water to boil, with the soul subjected to the danger of being scalded thereby.

So the graph of the soul's descent and return swings down from the fire-height of AB to MN and there turns back upward to end in the final letter. It may be a chance circumstance, but is at any rate an odd one, that if we start with A and then take in succession the final letter of the English alphabet, Z, the final one of Greek, O, and the final of the Hebrew, TH, it gives us the word AZOTH, the word used in Medieval "alchemy" to denote the primogenetic source-essence of life. If it were thus made up of the first and last letters of the three most representative alphabets it would have been intended to denote that basic essence which constitutes the substance of all life from the first step in creation through to the final dissolution of all things.

In descending from the height of fire essence to the depth of water substance, the energization would have had to pass through the intermediate stage or form of air. Fire symbolizes pure energy of spirit; air typifies mind; water stands for emotion, as earth for sensation in the scale of conscious states. If any of the letters between A and M are intended to mark the air stage, it has not come to knowledge as yet, unless it be that the bent form of the tenth

24

letter YOD, indicating the candle flame bent by a puff of air to denote the original impulse of God's mind on the flame, is to be taken in this significance.

M and N, separate or conjoined, form the framework of hundreds of words relating to the condition of spirit-energy when immersed in matter. As the primal mind-fire is the *father*, AB, so the primal matter-essence is the eternal *mother*, which in Hebrew is AM. M will be found to begin virtually all words denoting motherhood. M represents three, or five, or seven waves of water, and it should not be a matter of surprise, therefore, that we find all life on the planet having its generation in and from the sea water. Sea water is in a sense still the mother of our life, because that life is sustained by the electro-dynamic potencies in our blood, which is still chemically undistinguishable from sea water! Our blood *is* the red sea water! So we get the mother-name by conjoining the letter of potential fiery energy A, with matter symbolized by water, M. Our colloquial "Ma" for *mother* is essentially the Hebrew AM.

Starting with A M for *mother*, there is met an almost endless list of words whose connotations link them to the matter side of the life duality. To view them in the light of this orientation of thought is to discern in them new and vivid intimations of esoteric meaning. These recondite connotations can best be seen by contrasting their sense with their antonyms denoting fire, spirit and the fatherhood. To begin with, the creative powers symbolized by the letters at the head of the alphabet are *gods*; while the being who embodies god-power in matter is—*MaN*. The divine powers at the summit are unmanifest; in matter they become *MaNifest*. At the summit there is but *one* power, undifferentiated; below in matter it has *multiplied* itself and become the *MaNy*. At the god-height the power is purely spiritual; at the lower level it comes out as *MeNtal*; spirit above, *MiNd* below. At the top there is the maximum of power, even though purely potential; at the lower range it is *MiNus*, or at a *MiNimum*, though actual in its limited expression. A *man* is the cosmos in *MiNiature*. That which is expressed down here is, in comparison with the superior potential above, *MeaN*. Also as here the two poles of being are locked in a more or less stable equilibrium, things here are at a *MeaN* or *MediaN* counterbalance. To hold this steady is to *MaiNtain* life in its right poise. The father-power, AB is the conscious cognitive element in creation; the power it wields in matter, the M N energy of the atom, is the *MaNipulative* hand of God (the meaning of YOD); and so it is that the word for *hand* in many languages is not only compounded of M and N (Latin *manus*, Spanish *mano*, French *main*), but is in all languages *feminine* in gender, intimating the motherhood. In contrast to heaven above, the earth below is, in Latin, *MuNdus*, from which is our adjective *MuNdane*. Also from this comes *MouNt*, *MouNtain*, *MouNd*, already explained as referring to no hill on earth, but to the earth itself. Hebrew name for this lower vale of tribulation was *HiNNoM*, or *GehiNN- oM*. In the upper realms souls are not sufficiently individualized to deserve specific differentiated names; here soul gets its proper *NaMe*. The fate allotted to each soul by karmic desert comes out to *man*ifestation here below; it is therefore the soul's *NeMesis*. The soul here is under law, in Greek *NoMos*. A section of the terrain of a nation was by the Egyptians termed a *NoMe*. Since matter, like type-symbol, water, is, from the philosophical view of reality, nothing (it was designated by the Greeks "privation"), the Egyptian base-root of the letter N, whose hieroglyph was seven waves of water, along with the primal deific trinity *Nu, Nun, Nut*, gives us all the words expressing *Negation: no, not, neither, nor, none, nil, nix* (German: *nichts*), Latin *nox* (*night*), our *night, deny, neuter, never, nay*, German *nein, niemals*, etc., etc. Applied to man, his (relative) nothingness would make him "no one" which is in Latin *NeMo*. As man is cut off from deity here below, he is in Greek *MoNos, alone*. Also he is a *MoNad*. Perhaps *MoNk* is one who is alone, not united to the female counterpart.

The food the soul eats on earth is that divine *MaNNa* that was rained down from heaven, but had to be scraped up off the earth, the perfect analogue of how mortals acquire their heavenly nutriment. The universal ancient tribal name for the divinity manifesting in the life of nature was *MaNa, MaiNu, MaNitou*. Then we have the word for the thinking principle, which in the Hindu system is *MaNas*. One caught under the demoniac possession of this power was a *MaNiac*. In India the practice of prophecy was called *MaNtric* science. And the *-mon* in the word *deMoN* is probably of this derivation. The Greek Furies were called *MaeNads*. Plate refers to divine obsession as a *MaNia* better than sober reason. An *oMeN* was a foresight of one's earthly fate. And the mystifying and baffling word ending prayers, *aMeN*, if not directly from the Egyptian god of that same name, would seem by letter intimation to mean "so let it be," indicating that what is set forth should come to reality in the evolutionary process measured by the descent of soul into matter the whole way from A to M-N. *Memory* in Latin is *MeMiNi* and the Greek Muse of Memory was *MNemosyne*. To recall one's past is to *reMiNisce*. Things here are the *MiNutiae* of what is whole and integral above. They are *MiNute* in magnitude and last but a *MiNute* of time, poetically speaking.

Another most important line of derivatives branches off into sidereal regions. The great cosmic symbol, if not the embodiment of divine energy, is the sun. In contrast with its mighty generative power, its opposite character in the earthly region of the heavens, dead, inert, purely passive and reflective, the symbol of matter, is the *MooN*. Hence the composition of its name in English from M and N, giving also *MoNth*, *MoNday* and *MeNses*. If in Latin L stands for the divine Light, their *Luna* (the *moon*) might have taken form from the idea that on the lunar orb the divine Light (L) was weakened and dimmed by reflection from the surface of the negative lifeless moon, giving them LuNa, L for the light and N for the darkness; or it might have been originally L reflected in M-N, suggesting *LuMNa*, later wearing down into *Luna*. Oddly enough the Latin for *light* in its pure solar glory is *lux*; but for *light* in its earthly refracted dimmed form the word was *LuMen*. At any rate L and N are set directly at opposite nodes to each other in *lux, light*, and *nox* (Greek *nux*) *night*. L evidently here carries the connotation of divine character analyzed earlier. For not only does the Latin have *lumen* (our *illumine*) for *light*, but it has the word representing the divine light or power in things, *NuMen*, which comes close to bearing the same significance as *NoMen*, Latin for *name*.

The soul was thought to put on its bodily vesture as a *MaNtle*, which, as being the house it lived in was its *MaNse* or *MaNsion*. That which trailed back from the horse's head was his *MaNe*. That which flowed forth from the head of being was the *eMaNation* of creative force. The divinity implanted in living nature, most evolved in *man*, was *iMMaNent*, our *EMaNuel*.

It is close to certainty that here is to be found an explanation of a prominent item in the grammar of language, which seems still unknown in philological science, —the reason why the accusative (objective) case of all Latin nouns masculine and feminine in the singular number ends in the letter—M, and those corresponding in Greek end in —N, as also in Sanskrit and doubtless other languages. It is obvious that the M and N endings here denote *objectivity*, as the accusative is the objective case. Why this is so is definitely implicit in the significance of the meaning structure which places the two letters ending this case at the bottom of the descending arc of involution.

For the divine light is emanated from the supernal kingdom of spirit, and spirit is the active generative productive force that energizes all life process. It alone is self-generating, it alone initiates and institutes action. It is the father principle; the maternal-material principle is eternally only passive, receptive, mothering that which it receives germinally in its womb. The spirit force must stand as the actor; it does whatever is done; it moves upon the inert water, stirs them into agitation and motion to throw them into the forms of the conceived pattern. It is therefore the *subject* of the sentence that tells what its action initiates in the creative order. It is therefore in the *nominative* case, the subject-actor in the movement, and is grammatically called *nominative* because it gives specific character and *name* (Latin: *nomen*) to that which the action creates.

But what of the end product that the action brings into the status of being? As end product, materially created, it stands there as the *object* of the action, the thing purposed and by an energizing process made objective as the result. It is therefore the objective in view in the initial action and the objective thing produced. It must therefore be put into the *objective* case in grammar. The actor works subjectively, in the purely noumenal or subjective realm of conscious being. But its work is to bring its purposes thus subjectively conceived out into objective actuality. Hence the creative subject force that emanates out of the A B condition of primal being ends by generating its product here below at the M-N station of physical *objectivity*. The M and N terminations (even this word has the two letters in its context) therefore fitly appertain to the objective case of nouns, and the Latin, Greek, Sanskrit and others so have it. To illustrate the point, the nominative case of "trumpet" in Latin is *tuba*, but the objective case is *tubam*. So all nouns. Only in the case of neuter nouns is there no distinction between the nominative and accusative cases, obviously because a noun of neuter gender can not manifest any difference between subjective and objective status. It is not living, therefore can neither initiate action or be acted upon by its own volition, hence can be neither subject nor object in the living sense. The spiritually noumenal world is the realm where the subject principle initiates action; the lower physical world is the place where that action results terminally in the production of objectivity. M and N seem thus always to designate objectivity, and that again must be the reason for the composition of that English suffix denoting a thing's attain*ment* or achieve*ment* of its status of being in objectivity —*ment*.

The principle of explanation thus established is seen with startling definiteness in three of our common English personal pronouns. Of the first personal pronoun the nominative case is I, but the objective introduces the M: *me*. The third personal pronoun masculine singular is in the nominative *he*; but in the objective it is *him*. The third person plural nominative is *they*; but the objective is *them*. It is in passing to be noticed that the I is the only one of the pronouns capitalized, in respect to divinity, since the I-ego is the only part of us that is divine! Likewise the survival of the dot above the I (and the J) is the remnant of the YOD, the Hebrew divine flame. All this induces us to think that the I element (another word incidentally showing the L-M-N sequence) of a person is the subjective divine self within, initiating all action; while the outer personal physical bodily self is what this I has produced as the *me*. It might be said that the I has objectified itself in and as the *me*. What the noumenal I came to be when manifested outwardly in matter is the *me*. The I revealed itself in the *me*, just as it is said in religion that God has revealed or *ma*nifested himself to the world and in the world as Jesus. The ancients personalized a goddess named *Echo*. She represented the physical material repercussion to the impact of the waves of creative noumenal energy, the "voice" of God, upon matter. What matter, so to say, responded or answered was the "echo" of the divine voice. There is aptness and beauty in these ancient conceptions and ingenious allegorizations and poetizations once their sane high relevance is captured. The *me* is the echo from the side of matter of the divine voice of the I-ego.

The M is conspicuously seen as marking the point of lowest descent and beginning of return in a notable key-word in Hebrew.

The word for *sun* holds as high a place of glory in religious philology as does the radiant orb itself in the solar system. It typifies for mental illumination the same generative ray of power that its physical beams represent in the stellar cosmos. The Hebrew word for it was obviously aimed at embodying the story of its nature and its daily course of (apparent) travel. In outward semblance it appears as a globe of fiery essence that plunges at every eventide down into earth, or water, crosses a land of darkness and arises again unquenched in fiery splendor the following morning. As a globe of fire its nature would be expressed most fittingly by the letter *shin* (SH), with its threefold candle flame, the three YODS, above; the place of water into which it nightly descends would be indicated by M, and the place of its final return, the empyrean above, by SH again. So the word thus constituted would turn out to be SH-M-SH (*shemesh*); and this is just what it is. It is the old basic story of divine fire plunging down into water, the universal trope-figure under which all operation of spirit in and upon matter was dramatized.

It seems unquestioned that the Scriptural names of Samson, Saul, Samuel, Samael, Simeon, Simon, Solomon were based on this *semesh* stem. For all the divine figures in ancient spiritual dramas were essentially sun-god characters, typifying the spiritual aspect of the solar effluence in man. Samson's loss of power through the betrayal of Delilah fairly closely parallels Jesus' loss of life and his helplessness on the cross through his betrayal by Judas. Jesus, like Samson, was shorn of his aureole of glory which was replaced by the black crown of thorns, as Samson's loss of hair—always typical of solar rays—reduced him to impotency. And the etymology of *Delilah* is most significant as fulfilling her part in the allegory. In the case of Jesus' crucifixion "darkness was over the earth" during the agony. The name *Delilah* is compounded of the Hebrew word for *night*, *lilah* (*lailah*), with the fourth Hebrew letter, D, prefixed. Now the tribe of Dan was in astrological tropism allocated to the autumn sign of Scorpio, when the sun is entering the winter-time of darkness and solar feebleness. So Scorpio was called the gate or door of the dark "underworld," which in the Egyptian was named the *Tuat*, now tending to be spelled also with a D, as *Duat*, *Duad*. When we turn to the Hebrew alphabet and see that D, *daleth*, means *door*, we have the name *D-lilah* reading definitely "the door of the dark underworld of night." This may seem far-fetched to those not habituated to the nature of ancient allegorical composition of spiritual myths. When the name of a paramour of a sun-god figure works out to mean the "door of the dark night" of incarnation, the fitness of the construction is most astonishingly convincing and clearly reflects a designed conception.

When one encounters and unravels not only one or two chance constructions of this kind, but scores of them, indeed finds them at every turn, one is certain that the methodology of ancient cryptic writing has been rediscovered. When this disclosure is carried through to the farthest limit of its bearings on the significance of the ancient literature, it is recognized with astonishment that the meaning-content of archaic writing was expressed as definitely by the form-structure of the material as by the connotation of the words. It is becoming more clearly discerned that the formulators of the sacred scripts of antiquity strove to dramatize a postulated form of cosmic structure in a graph outlining the life development and movement by imitating its rhythms and number counts, its cyclical swirls and sweeps, in the organic form of the textual construction. Thus it is seen that the numerical basis of Bible writing in Old Testament Hebrew and New Testament Greek is the "magic" number *seven*. The number value of thousands of verses, divine names, key phrases and even whole Bible books is with surprising regularity a multiple of seven. Thus there are seven Hebrew words in the first verse of *Genesis;* and some ten or twelve other combinations in the verse score multiples of seven. Life, so to say, in every one of its creative advances travels in seven-league boots, dances to a seven-beat measure, runs a scale of seven notes. It is evident that the authors of Holy Writ labored to inweave the form of this movement into the writing itself. The lilt and swing of Bible poetry, the elements of rhythm, meter, cadence and pause, is to reproduce in mantric value the lilt and swing of evolution itself. That this methodology has lain under the eye of scholarship for these twenty centuries or more without its implications being seen or guessed is unimpeachable testimony to the blindness of religious obsession.

Another most significant combination of the divine SH with the earthly M-N comes to view in the Hebrew word for *oil, shemen.* Here the fire-symbol, SH, is united with both the water letters. As the fuel for fire and the substance used in the divine anointing, which is itself the dramatization of the divinizing of man, oil is one of the most frequent symbols of the deific power in the Scriptures and mythology. The great divine names *Christ* and *Messiah* both mean "the Anointed One."

It was observed earlier that when the X symbol of the developing movement of creation was lifted out of the matter-symbol O and placed after it, we strangely found that it spelled the word OX. This singular circumstance at once bred the conviction that this word, this theriograph, or animal hieroglyph, should play some prominent part in the scheme of ancient figurative representation of values and relations. It was of course known to be a figure in a number of Biblical stereotypes as well as in Greek and other mythic stories. But its full symbolic import was not realized until the significance of its connection with the first letter of the Hebrew alphabet came to view with startling impact. *Aleph*, A, has for its name coefficient this very word OX. Along with this, there is also the Hebrew letter L, *lamed*, with the meaning of *ox-goad*.

But why is A denominated by the ox-symbol? What is the significance of this animal that connects it with the first letter? Revelation of this profound and recondite symbolism should indeed open the eyes of all Scriptural exegetists to the almost impenetrable crypticism of ancient esoteric writing, which they have with such obdurate intransigence continued to deny, ignore and scorn.

To put it in the most compact form of statement, it appears that A was denominated the ox because, as the animal is unproductive, incapable of begetting life—as the result of desexing—so the primal state or stage of creation, represented by the latter A, is unproductive, incapable of begetting life. The alphabet's first character fittingly represents the no-not-nought-nothing stage of the cyclical creation. It is the pre-zoic stage, the lingering darkness before the first rays of dawn. As yet there is nothing, neither matter nor movement. It is the absolute zero on life's or the cycle's thermometer. It is the state which the Egyptians described by their name NU (NUN, NUT), *night*, and the Hebrews by their AIN. It is the stage when naught was. In it nothing could be produced, nothing could have birth. It was the great darkness, the great deep, into whose bosom had not yet fallen the seminal seed of new creation. It was sheer potential of life, standing, like the ox, unfertilized, unimpregnated by the fructifying ray of cosmic mind, impotent to mother life until so enriched.

If this seems like an arbitrary fancy, it also appears to be indubitably substantiated by the positive fact that in the main languages, from Sanskrit down to English, this letter A is the universal prefix which gives to all words with which it is conjoined the *negative* meaning. It can be translated invariably by the word "not." In Greek it is called "*alpha privative*," the letter that *deprives* a word of its positive meaning, making it negative. A-theist, a-gnostic, a-symmetrical, a-moral, a-mnesia, a-pathetic, a-tom (not cuttable), even the Greek word for "truth," *a-letheia*, (that which is not forgotten), and a host of others attest the negative force of A.

This being so, we are introduced directly to another outstanding fact in connection with the succeeding letter, the second of the alphabet, B. It is not by chance or as a pure pun that *begin* begins with B. For in the structural formation of the alphabet, since the creation does *not* begin with A, a pre-creation stage, the ancient books definitely state that it starts with B, —B-gins, as it were. B is therefore the first letter in the actual creation. How fitting it is, then, that it is the first letter of the first verse of *Genesis*, which starts with the Hebrew word *b,rashith* and that followed by the verb *bara*. *B, rashith* means *in the beginning* and *bara* means *created*. Yes, creation begins with B, not a-gins with A. As the beginning institutes the process of coming to *be*, or *becoming*, these words also start with B. The great number of German words with the prefix *be-*, as *bekommen, bekennen, bedenken*, and a very large number also in English, as *beget, betoken, bespeak, besmirch, behave* and *befriend*, all carry the meaning of a movement coming, so to say, to a becoming. And in what way could the whole process of creation be more graphically expressed than by saying that it is a movement on its way to becoming to be? As the great Hindu philosopher Aurobindo expresses it, "the only being is becoming." Can it be without significance, then, that the Hebrew word meaning *to come* is just the B leading out the A, —BA? And this also spells the Egyptian word meaning the soul that *comes to being* here in the body. And would it be sheer coincidence that our *born, bear, birth, breed, baby, beget*, all start with B? And that *well* or *spring* in Hebrew is *baer*? (*Beer Sheba*, "*the well of the seven*.") We cry Abba father, says the Scripture, which, if *ab* is *father*, and *ba* means *comes*, would have us saying "the father comes"—in the character of his Christly Son on earth, the ray in us of the Father principle in the universe.

It may be asked, why, since the tenth letter YOD represents the flame of the divine creative fire, and indeed gives its name to *God*, the *shin* (S or SH) has come in for so much of the divine fire symbolism. Our answer can not be categorical or dogmatic. It can be speculated that as the YOD represented the flame in its primal oneness, the *shin* represented it when it had differentiated into the triplicity, for it contains three YODS. It does not seem a wild assumption to think also that the letter chosen to carry the hissing sound of S and SH should depict the threefold divine fire, for the fire became triple only when it entered the watery composition of the body, and the S and SH sound is precisely that produced by fire plunging into water! The YOD then can be taken as representing the cosmic fire when first fanned by the breath of God. Jesus is dramatized as coming "with his fan in his hand" to generate heat to mold the worlds in proper shape and to fan into bright flame the smoldering fire of divinity in man's constitution. *Shin* would represent the fire, now become triple, plunging into the lower levels of water, standing both for the actual water of the human body and as a general symbol of matter. The three YODS of the *shin* have lines carrying their power down to the bottom level, where they are united in one common bar, this again intimating that the three divine aspects, spirit, soul and mind, are all mingled as one in the body of man. As a symbol designed to depict the immersion of fiery spiritual units of consciousness in their actual baptism in the water of physical bodies, the letter form that dramatizes the actual event, and the letter sound that onomatapoetically mimics the sound of fire plunging into water, this alphabet character *shin* is certainly most eloquently suggestive.

It has often been said that the S (SH) sound is derived from the *hiss* of the serpent. This tradition seems more likely to have come from the ancient symbolism of fire plunging into water (symbol of soul descending into body) than from the inaudible "hiss" of the snake. For, again coincidental as it may seem, the creative fire was by the ancients called the "serpent fire," expressly by the Egyptians the great *uraeus* snake, "a serpent of fire."

Let it be noted also with regard to the *shin*, that when a dot— likely acting deputy for the YOD—is placed above the *right* side of the letter, it is pronounced as SH; but when the dot comes above the *left* side, it has only the sound of S. This change of position of the dot actually changes the name of the letter; for when it is above the left side, the name is not *shin*, but *sin*. Doubtless a thunder of protest and a charge of scholarly chicanery would greet our intimation that this left-handed name of the great divine letter is the origin and covertly carries the significance of the theological word *sin*. What can be adduced in some support of the suggestion is not without considerable force on that side. There is the Bible phrase, "the wilderness of Sin," which is the same as the "wilderness of Sin-ai," and the "mount of Sin," which our study so far alone has shown to be the "mount of the earth," i.e., the earth itself, as that celestial mount on which every transaction of the business of human divinization takes place.

A salient feature of the ancient science of truth representation was the designation of things spiritual and divine as allocated to the *right* side of life and things mundane and physical as of the *left* side. Good lay on the right hand, evil on the left. Esotericism has always spoken of the right and the left-hand path. Such books as the *Zohar* and other haggadic works of the early Jewish allegorists prominently use this figurism. To go left, to stand on the left, was to "miss the mark" of good and truth and right. The Greek word for *to sin* is precisely this: *hamartano*, "to miss the mark." The sharp distinction between the two directions has always appeared even in language with a moral connotation. The Latin word for right hand is *dexter*, from which we get *dexterous*; the French is *droit*, from which comes *adroit*. For left hand the Latin has our own word *sinister*; the French has *gauche*, from which comes our *gawky*. Things on the right were favorable, propitious; on the left were sinister, ill-omened. And as St. Paul's Epistles (mainly *Romans* 7) so pointedly reveal, earth was that mount on which the divine soul, sinless in its celestial habitation, came under the dominion of sin. "Know ye not, my brethren," asks the Apostle, "how that a man is under the law (of *sin* and death) only as long as he liveth?"—that is, while he is here on earth. He implies that there is no sin in heaven, for he clearly states that "sin sprang to life" when the soul obeys the "command" to incarnate. Sin can touch the soul only from the side of body, and, he says, the soul goes "dead" under its power while here on earth until its resurrection "from the dead" in the course of evolution of spirit back to its divine condition. So that the earth is that "Mount of Sin," that "Mount Sin-ai" of the Scriptures.

But the Old Testament contains an allegory—for the story is preposterous as history—which shows the ancient writers of

35

sacred ideological constructions using the *shin-sin* difference to point the moral that the soul that can pronounce the full SH sound of the letter has taken the *right* path and completed its evolution to divinity; while the one that can enunciate only the S sound has taken the left-hand path to "sin" and must return to earth, the land of "death" for further schooling in life. The guards at the Jordan fords were instructed to subject the Ephraimites on the east side of Jordan who wished to cross to enter the Holy Land (not of Judea, but of spiritual consciousness) to a simple test: require each man who crosses to pronounce the key word *Shibboleth*. But, says the story, in every case "he said *Sibboleth*." The direful result was that forty-two thousand Ephraimites who could not convert the S indicating *sin* into the divine SH were put to the sword on one day. They were still on the left-hand path of *sin*, not yet ready to "cross the river" into the land of spiritual blessedness.

It seems worthy of remark that not in twenty centuries has the easy esoteric unraveling of this simple and evident cryptogram come through to the intelligence of any scholar. How a Hebrew exegetist could long miss it is not comprehensible. Furthermore, how it could have been mistaken for history, for an actual event, is still far more incomprehensible. Yet Fundamentalists still claim that it "happened." If you assert that "history" was only a few thousand years ago a run of miracles, of course it neither needs nor can have an explanation. One is just to gape in awe at the Lord's wondrous doings and be sanctified of soul, —if stultified of mind.

If the S and SH sounds carried the intimation of fire plunging into water, a special use of these letters in the old Egyptian hieroglyphic language seems to fall into conformity with the same idea. The S (SH) was consistently prefixed to verbs to express the idea of setting off the action which the verb indicated, to give the action its initial push, or s-tart, as it were. The likelihood of the origin of this usage from the basic fire-going-into-water thesis will not so hastily be scouted if it is reflected that in the creation no real beginning in the visible worlds can have been made until the fire of spirit potency has radiated forth from the divine thought and impregnated the sea of matter (water.) The visible and audible work of creation starts only when the two nodes of being approach each other and establish tensional relation between themselves. As many a scientific speculator has predicted, the early stages of earth's formation brought together the chemical elements of fiery gases and humid vapors, the precipitates from the mixture finally forming the first earthly and mineral substances. Those early periods might, in the Egyptian sense, be termed the hissing, or S (SH) stage of planetary evolution.

An example of the inceptive force of the S in the hieroglyphics is seen in the Egyptian word MNKH (MeNKH), which as adjective means *firm, stable*. But, made into a verb, it becomes SMNKH (SMeNKH), meaning to *make firm, stabilize, establish*. It is also likely that in this word MeNKH we have another prime example of the M-N reference. In relation to its meaning of firmness and stability, it is to be recalled that a passage from the Egyptian *Book of the Dead* described this world of life on earth as "the place of establishing forever." Also in the M-N connection it is highly significant that the Egyptian name for this lower region, the "underworld" or "nether earth" of their system, was *Amenta*, composed of the name of the God *Amen* and *ta*, meaning *earth*. Also significant is the name of this god, made up of the A and the M and N, for he was called "the god in hiding," and his hieroglyph is a god seated under a canopy. Obviously he then is the personification of the divine nature hidden under the canopy of our mortal flesh.

All this should be a specific guiding datum for philosophical science, inasmuch as orthodox theology has loaded the evolutionary marshland, or Reed Sea, of the earthy-watery human body with heavy contumely as the place where only fleeting ephemeral influences affect, if not afflict, the soul with evil. That it is, on the contrary, the place where the soul establishes forever its grounding in fundamental realities, is a tenet of the sacred and secret wisdom of the Egyptian sages which must be made one of the chief stones in the new temple of rational religion now in process of building.

The S prefixed to MNKH adds the starting force that brings the firm establishing to actuality, that sets it to work. It is hardly unlikely that the very long run of English verbs which begin with S (or SH) carry this inceptive or initiating force of the letter—though speculation of this sort can not be asserted with too much certainty—in such words as *start, step, slide, shake, skip, skate, slip, sink, stir, sneak, smite, spur, shout, scream, stamp, stand, spit, slap, shoot, speak, sprint, spurn, scoff, slay, spill, sift* and scores more.

Massey traces even the great name of mystery, the *sphinx*, from the ANKH stem, preceded by the demonstrative adjective P (*this, the, that*) and the starting S, thus: S-P-ANKH. Massey was well versed in the abstrusities of the hieroglyphics and his surmise on this is as good as that of others. The word thus composed would mean "the beginning of the process of linking spirit and matter," which indeed is the sphinx-riddle of the creation. The sphinx image does conjoin the head of man, spirit, with the body of the animal, lion, representing matter. It is precisely such values and realities that the sages of antiquity dealt with and in precisely this manner of subtle indirection. When will modern scholarship come to terms with this recognition!

If *sphinx* derives from the ANKH symbol, it is not at all unlikely that the other great emblem suggestive of the spirit involved in matter, the wondrous "bird of life," the *phoenix*, stems from it likewise. It was also named the *bennu*, the spirit energy that goes from B, the fiery start, down into water, N, which is also probably the make-up of the Hebrew word for *son*, which is *ben*. Another name of the fabled bird was *nycticorax*. *Corax* is *raven* in Greek, which, from its black color, is often called the "bird of night," symbolizing the soul flying down into the dark night of imprisonment in earthly bodies; and *nycti* stems from the Greek *nux* (*nyx*), meaning *night*. The mythic phoenix was pictured as migrating north and returning south (to Egypt), where it renewed its life in death from the germinal worm surviving in its ashes. The soul likewise migrates "north" to heaven and "south" to earth in periodic rhythm. And "Egypt" is symbolically the earth. Can there be doubt that the fabled migratory fowl is just the divine soul of life that commutes regularly between heaven and earth, pictured as a bird because it can build a nest on the ground, but equally well rise into the heavens of consciousness?

It would be highly revealing to recapitulate some of the, at times, astonishing formulations which the ancient Hebrews discovered as fortuitous or designed constructions in their interpretative methodology that was elementary to their so-called science of Gematria. This was based on the equation of number value of the words with the meanings expressed in the text. The number-forms were held to "geometrize," so to say, the meanings. As a physical object or phenomenon can configurate a meaning structure so can number values and relations. This "science" was carried to

38

lengths that have ever seemed to overrun the bounds of rational sense, and the method has been held in disdain as fantastic jugglery since the days of its esoteric vogue. Yet it would seem to be grounded on legitimate premises and to be subject to criticism only in its unwarranted extravagances. One senses this in reading the *Zohar*, for instance.

Somewhat in the spirit of the Gematria modus it may be profitable to look at several word and letter combinations in the Hebrew. To condense in a sentence what would take ten pages to elucidate in full, it is notable that beside the number of central and basic significance in this systematization, seven, perhaps the one most prominent in the sacred numerology was *six*. If seven was the number rounding out the cycles, six was the one that completed the *physical* evolution of the life-forms of any cycle. The progress achieved in the first six sub-cycles was necessary preparation for the channeling down of the *spiritual* grade in the seventh and climactic sub-cycle. We find the deeply esoteric Jewish philosopher Philo in the first century A. D. giving expression to the importance of the number six in several statements. One runs: "The world was created according to the perfect nature of the number six." And again he asks who can fittingly celebrate the divine majesty of this number. He says also that the sixth day of creation was the "festal day of all the earth." The creation was to work at physical labor for six days and rest in spiritual delight on the seventh. Man, made in the image and likeness of the cosmic creation, is likewise to work only six days in the analogical cycle of seven days.

Therefore the number six, hardly less than the number seven, furnishes the basic clue to the meaning-value of many words. As six stages finished the physical form of creation in any cycle, it would seem likely that the Gematria plan would have used the final letter or letters of the alphabet to construct the words carrying the value of six. We are not disappointed in our gematric expectations here, for the last three letters of the Hebrew alphabet are R, S (SH) and TH, and *six* is written variously *shesh*, *shisah*, *sheth* and *sixth* is *shishi*. It is likely that if records were available we should find that the last son of Adam in the *Genesis* had been traditionally regarded as the sixth, for his name is *Seth* or *Sheth*.

But the Hebrew Bible's very first word opens up a veritable mine of speculative possibilities of this sort. That first word, translated "in the beginning," is in Hebrew B'RASHITH. It was either constructed with amazing ingenuity to express a remarkable cosmographic conception or chanced to do just that by sheer coincidence. The reader must first be reminded that in the ancient manuscripts of the Biblical books the words were not separated and there were no vowels! It is therefore permissible to separate the words in different ways and in doing so some curious new readings come out as possibilities.

The initial B is a preposition meaning "in" and can be prefixed to any noun or participial verb. RASH means *head*, so that B'RASH would mean "in the head," "in his (God's) head," as the place where God "created the heaven and the earth." Oddly enough it is precisely in God's head that the creation started, as there were formed the archetypal ideas over the pattern of which he shaped the creation. If B'RASHITH might be considered the overlapped form of B'RASH-SHITH, it would read "in the head of the six" or "of the sixth," and again it can be said (and the *Zohar* expressly does say it) that the creation, emanating out of God's head, came to a head in the sixth formative impulsion.

Then B'RASHITH is followed by the verb BARA, "he created." If we take the B'RA for BARA (the vowels being wholly conjectural and indeterminable), BARASHITH itself would read "he created six, or the sixth." The *Zohar* gives this as a reading alternative. And it does in fact look as if this first Hebrew word was designedly made up of the first letter with which the creation truly begins, B, to indicate the beginning of the process, and the last *three* letters, R, SH and TH, to spell out, as it were, a cosmic evolution running clear through from beginning to end and so inscribed in the alphabet. The use of all three final letters would appear to indicate that the creative process brought out the result of the operation of the original unit divine mind manifesting in its triple aspects of spirit-soul-mind. The SH itself carries this triplicity, we have seen, in its three YODS. So that in its full esoteric sweep of meaning this first Bible word B'RASHITH would condense a far more comprehensive significance than its conventional translation would show. It would really read: "From the beginning in his head God unfolded from his triple powers of mind the heavens and the earth in six creative stages." This must stand as most likely the first full esoteric translation of the first Bible verse.

The Hebrew words for *water* and *heaven* will lucidly illustrate the water-value of M and the fire-value of SH. *Water* is MAYIM, the M conspicuously predominating. As the Y is another form of the fiery I, MAY (MAI) would read as the M-water expression of the I-fire power. Esoterically the universe can be thought of in just those terms. Now, most appropriately, the word for *heaven* is this same water-word, MAYIM, preceded by the SH of fire, SH'MAYIM. Earth is the home or world of water; heaven is the home of water generated by fire, —the lightning; or water as invisible vapor, or water proceeding out of the *empyrean*, or realm of potential fire. Jesus says that he beheld Satan as lightning, or fire, falling from heaven, and that he himself came "to send fire on the earth in the sight of men." The Greeks said that the gods "distribute the divine fire" among men, a portion of soul-fire to each. *Genesis* tells us that God first created the two firmaments in the midst of the waters, the firmament above and the firmament below, the MAYIM and the SH'MAYIM, the water and the fire-water.

Such a word as YOM, for *day*, seems to reveal semantic formation. The time-words, of whatever period, age, aeon, cycle, year, month, week, day, hour, are used very definitely to indicate no actual time-periods, but whole cycles as a concept, not a specific duration. A cycle is a *year*, a *day*, a *week*, a *month*. The world was created in six "days." The Israelites (again not the historical Hebrews) marched in the Sinai desert "forty days, for every day a year," says the text. So YOM (IOM) is the "day" of creation. It would be the period in which life proceeds from start at A (B) to deploy the creative fire-power, I (Y), into manifestation at M (N). This "day" would last from I (Y) to M, making its name YOM. As the action between A, or I (Y), and M (N) represents the process of life's coming to be, or becoming, it seems almost as if we find it saying I A M. Is it strange that the Latin word for *now* is IAM? It is as if life were saying "I am in existence in the eternal NOW." If one were to say "I am" in English and *now* in Latin, it would be *I am iam*. Coincidence it is, no doubt, but both forms must be composed of the same primal letter elements.

To say "I am" in German gives interesting results also. It is *Ich bin*. The *Ich* is the I heavily aspirated. In some parts of Germany the *Ich* is pronounced as *Ish*. This equates the Hebrew word for *man*, uniting the primal unitary I-fire-power with the triple manifestation of that power that the SH represents; and this is precisely what man does. In man the divine *trinity* comes to

41

manifestation. But the German, instead of using the pre-creative A and the matter-terminal M to say "am," says it with the *actual* beginning letter B and the other matter-terminal, N, with the I between them (as it does stand between them in the alphabet), giving BIN, *Ich bin.*

It is not to be forgotten that LOVE was one of the three elements in the great ANKH symbol, along with LIFE and TIE.. Now it is in the descent of soul fire from A (B) to M and back to the final letter (in Greek it is O) that the two poles of being generate the power of divine LOVE. Is it not a bit surprising, then, that to say in Latin "I love" is to say AMO?

The significance of the Hebrew word for "the oil of anointing," SHeMeN, has already been mentioned. Since this divine oil that, so to say, is destined to set the head of man on fire with the divine unction, manifests in man in its triple spirit-soul-mind divisions, it must be recognized as of great significance that repeatedly the Old Testament instructs that the sacrificial cakes are to be compounded of fine flour mixed with *three* measures of oil. The three divine flames that are to deify man are to be fed by the "oil" compressed out of the wine-press or olive-press of our conscious earthly experience.

It would be gratuitous to assert that the Hebrew *shemen, oil,* derived from the earlier Egyptian word *smen.* This was an incense spoken of in the Ritual for the dead, those "dead," however, being the souls incarnated in bodies on earth, and not the "shades" of deceased mortals. The word must therefore refer to an element in the human constitution, not of course, to be taken as an actual physical substance burning at funerals. In this connection it can be speculated whether the *Geth-* of *Gethsemane* is not a variant of *Beth* as in Bethel, Bethany, Bethlehem, meaning *house.* If so, the word *Gethsemane* would mean the house in which life burns its *smen*-incense to divinize its child, man; that "house" being man's physical body, the *beth* or home of souls on earth. It was in Gethsemane that the Christos wrestled in the living agony that caused "him" to sweat, as it were, great drops of blood. Several of the prime Egyptian mythic legends of the creation of mankind by the gods represent the deity as exuding drops of his blood *seminally* upon the earth, from which sprang the two characters, male and female, that equate Adam and Eve in the *Genesis* allegory. Seminal creative blood essence is more than a few times poetized as sweat.

All this is of epochal importance as demonstrating that the bloody sweat of Jesus in Gethsemane is a watered-down rescript of one of the old Egyptian mythic constructions.

It must strike any person of open mind how marvelously these words articulate in all these constructions with perfect naturalness and semantic felicity. The Scriptures have remained for centuries both a perplexing riddle and a derationalizing influence simply because the abstruse and recondite relevance of these symbolic terms has never hitherto been explored.

The study could be pursued to the dimensions of a major work. Enough has been given to answer the purposes of an introductory treatise that has been undertaken at the urgent behest of many who heard the exposition in lecture form. By way of epilogue and summary it will be well to end with the analysis of another pivotal Hebrew word of only two (Hebrew) letters, as it will provide virtually irrefutable certification of the main theses of this essay: the descent of spirit-fire into matter-water at the middle or nadir point of the alphabet, M-N, and its return. That little word is in Hebrew HAG (CHAG), base of the Mohammedan words *haj, hajj, hegira*. It is given in lexicons as meaning *feast, festal day, festival, holy day (holiday)*; also as *pilgrimage, journey, flight*. The Hebrews themselves seem to have little apprehension of its true significance, even on its exoteric side. What it connotes in its esoteric reference has never yet been given out. It is virtually the cryptic key to the Scriptures, the definite key to the *chiasmus* construction of much of the material in the Scriptures, in which verses or portions of chapters are arranged in the form of a succession of four separate statements made successively in a line outward, so to say, as A, B, C, D and then a return back over the same first three, C, B, A, giving a seven-form structure, A, B, C, D, C, B, A. It seems to put the seven-stage structure in the form of an outgoing journey or pilgrimage, HAG, of three and a half steps or stages, and a return over the same three and a half, the turn to return (*Sinai* by Egyptian derivation) being made at the middle point of the fourth, or D, stage. To this structure the name *chiasmus* has been given, from the form of the Greek letter *chi* (much like our X), the two upper arms of which pictorialize a descent and return.

The HAG ordained by the Lord for Israelite observance in *Leviticus* reproduces the framework of this same design, though

43

here in the form or terms of a feast or festival ceremonial. Bu deeper research reveals that it was to be carried out in the form o an actual pilgrimage, setting out from home, journeying outwar for three and a half days, *crossing a river* or *water* boundary be tween two kingdoms, (and *always* crossing at that point,) and the the return. It was to be an actual march out, an *exodus* of thre and a half days, and the *nostos*, or return journey of equal lengtl The tradition of its meaning, preserved better in Mohammeda ideology than in Christian or Hebrew, was the origin of the Islami pilgrimage, the great *hegira* to Mecca; for that matter the origi of all religious pilgrimaging.

When we turn to the Scriptural *Book of Revelation*—and othe places—we are there faced with the recurrence of this specifi number, three and one-half (the half of seven!), *three* times in th eleventh and twelfth chapters of the last book in the Bible. Thi book, has twenty-two chapters, and, whether it be by chance o by design of ancient structure-builders of archaic literature, th eleventh and twelfth chapters stand at the place in the book cor responding to where M and N stand in the alphabet, —the middl or turning point. This would seem to indicate that the entire boo of twenty-two chapters was arranged with the intent to reproduc the chiasmus structure. That is, at the three-and-a-half point i the book the number three and a half is introduced three times!

It seems so clear as to be beyond cavil that this definite form was used in symbolism to dramatize the outgoing or descent o the soul into incarnation through three and a half root stages o matter, from ethereal to solid, its experience there in a body o (seven-eighths) water, and its evolutionary return through the same three and a half levels, reaping on its return its harvest o rich experience. Yet this, the open sesame to all the baffling mystery of Holy Writ, has eluded the sagacity of the Scriptural pundits for centuries. Most lucidly it allegorizes the soul's pil-grimage out or down to body, and its return. Most astonishing is the item that at the outward terminus of the three and a half "days" journey was a river or water body on the boundary between two kingdoms. This the soul had to cross to begin its return. If sufficient poetic imagination is used to see that this Red Sea—Jordan River—Styx River of the allegories is actually *the red blood of our human bodies*, the Scriptures begin at once to become like an opaque glass suddenly made transparent.

CPSIA information can be obtained at www.ICGtesting.com
Printed in the USA
BVOW09s1749031215

428873BV00005B/35/P